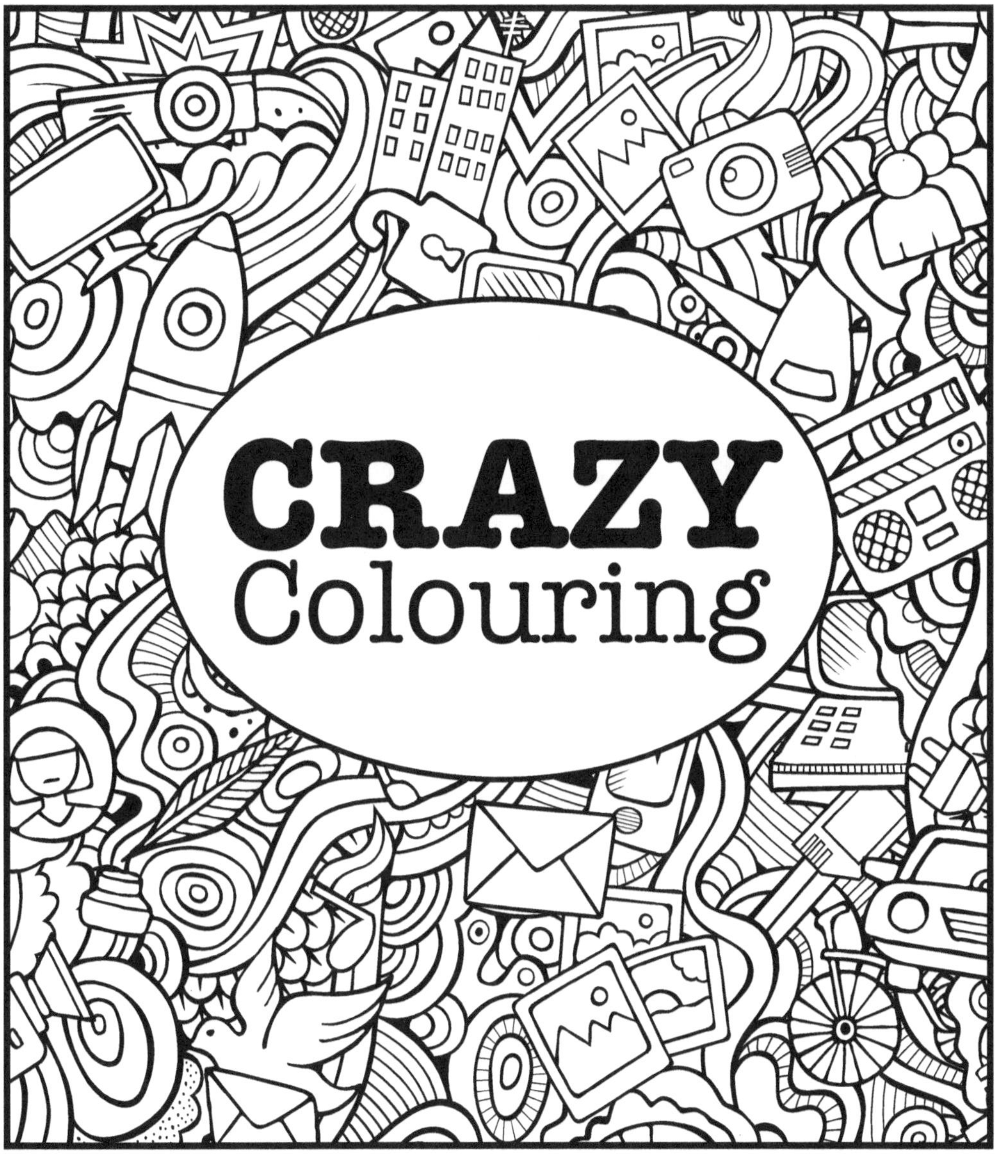

CRAZY Colouring

Brilliant Colouring For Boys **Book 2**

First published in 2016 by Kyle Craig Publishing

Editor: Alison McNicol

Design: Elizabeth James, Julie Anson, Alison McNicol, Shutterstock, Inc.

ISBN: 978-1-78595-126-8

A CIP record for this book is available from the British Library.

A Kyle Craig Publication

www.kyle-craig.com

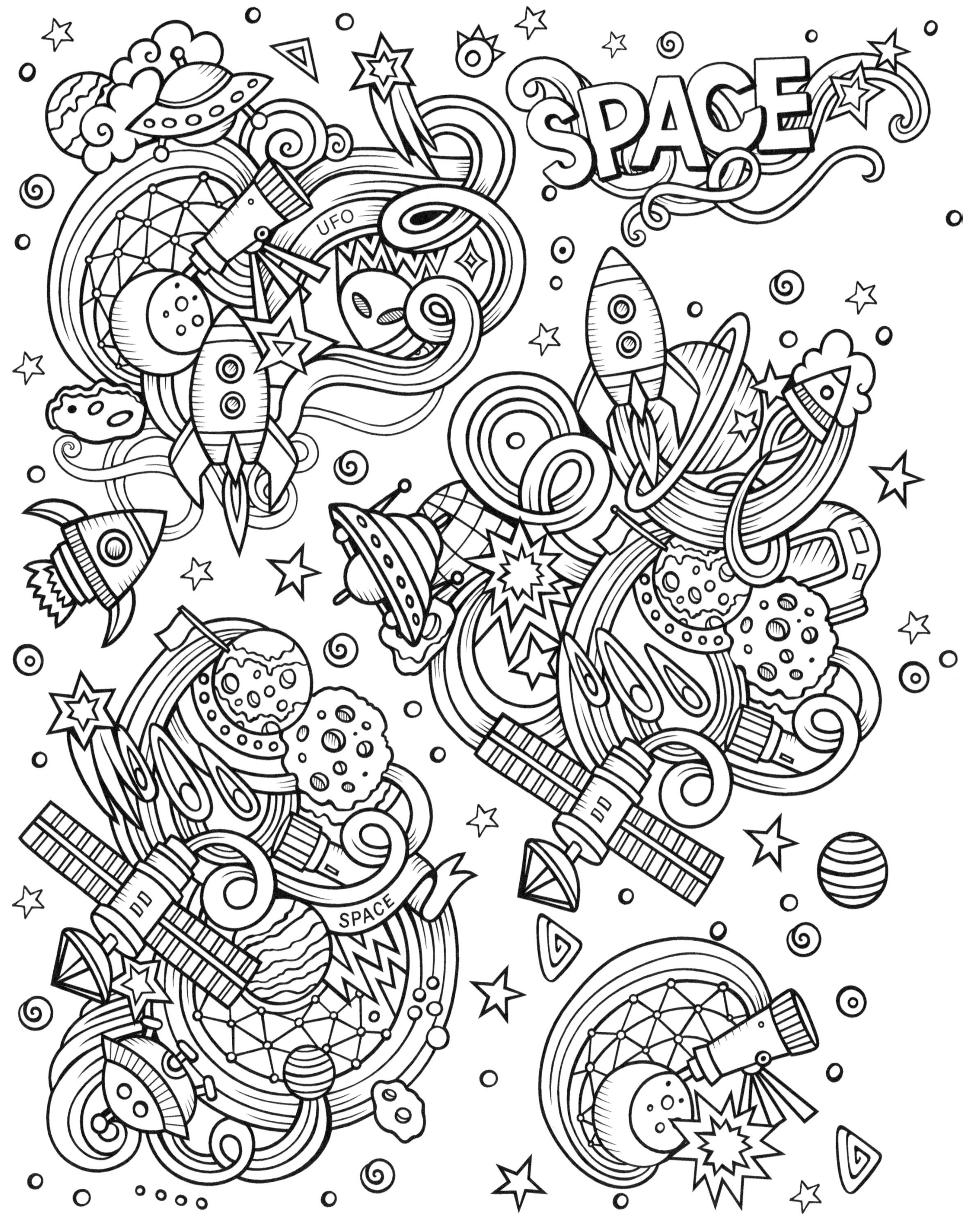
SPACE
UFO
SPACE

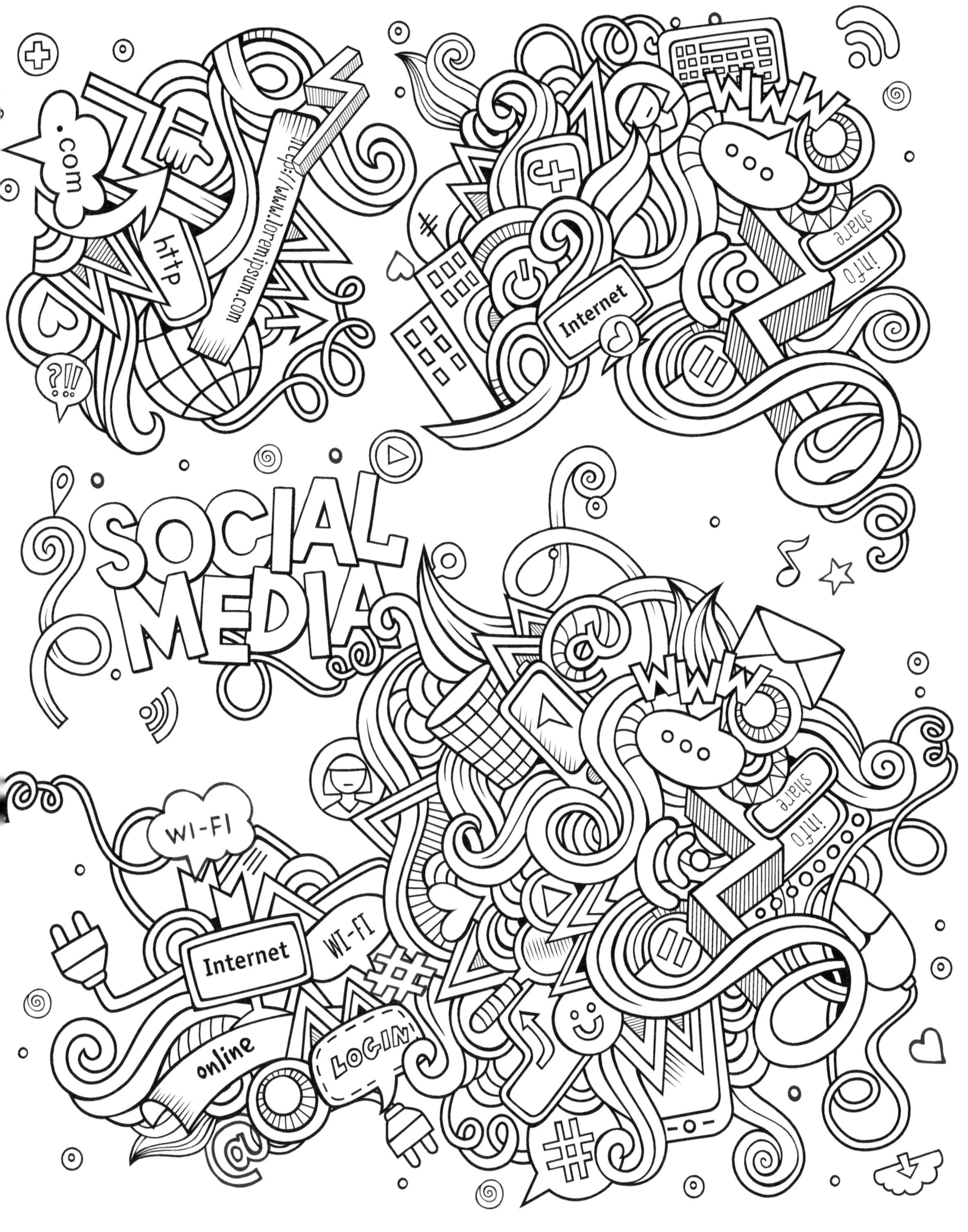

SOCIAL MEDIA
.com
http
http://www.loremipsum.com
www
share
info
Internet
WI-FI
Internet
WI-FI
online
LOGIN
www
share
info

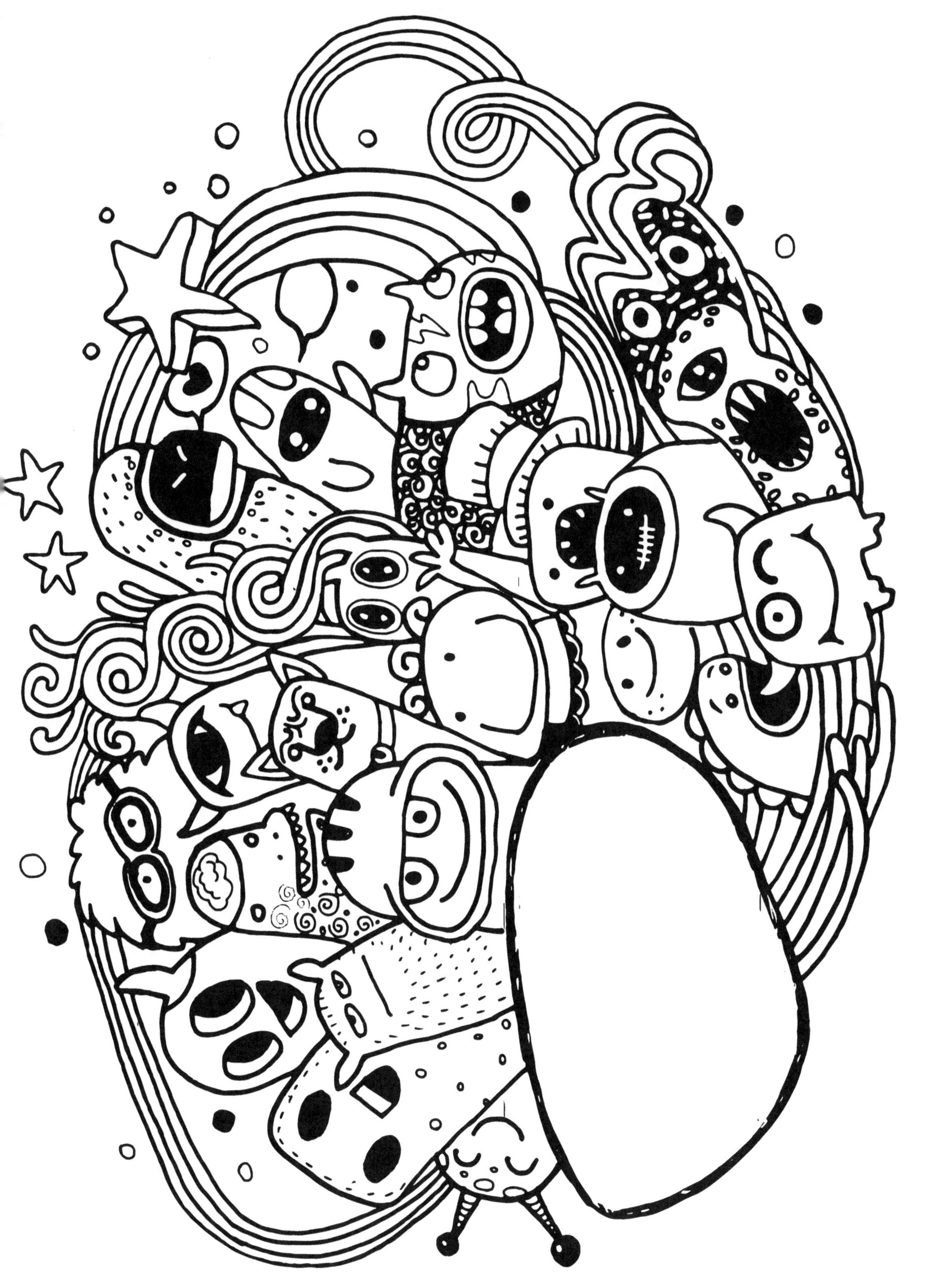

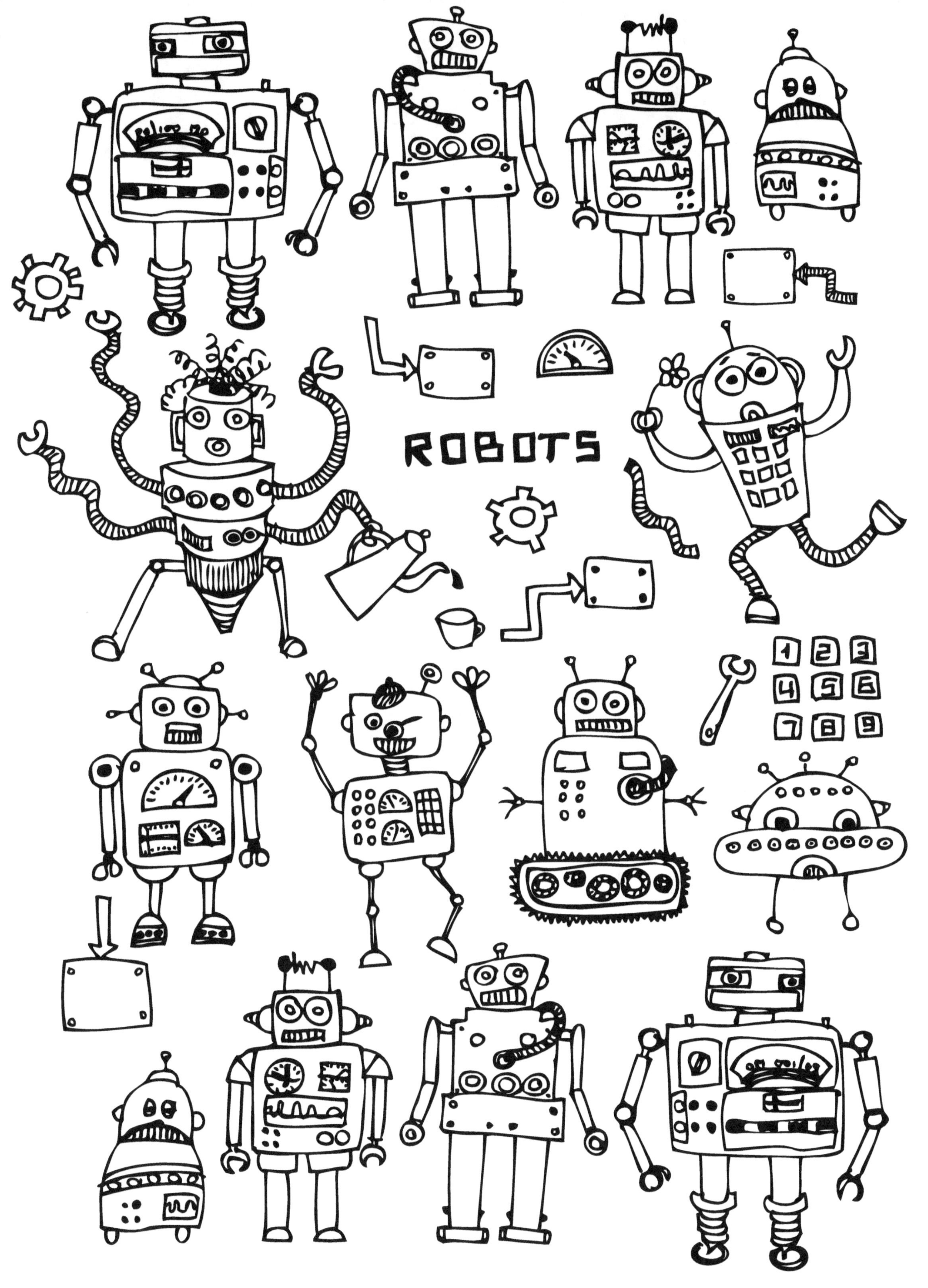
ROBOTS
1 2 3
4 5 6
7 8 9

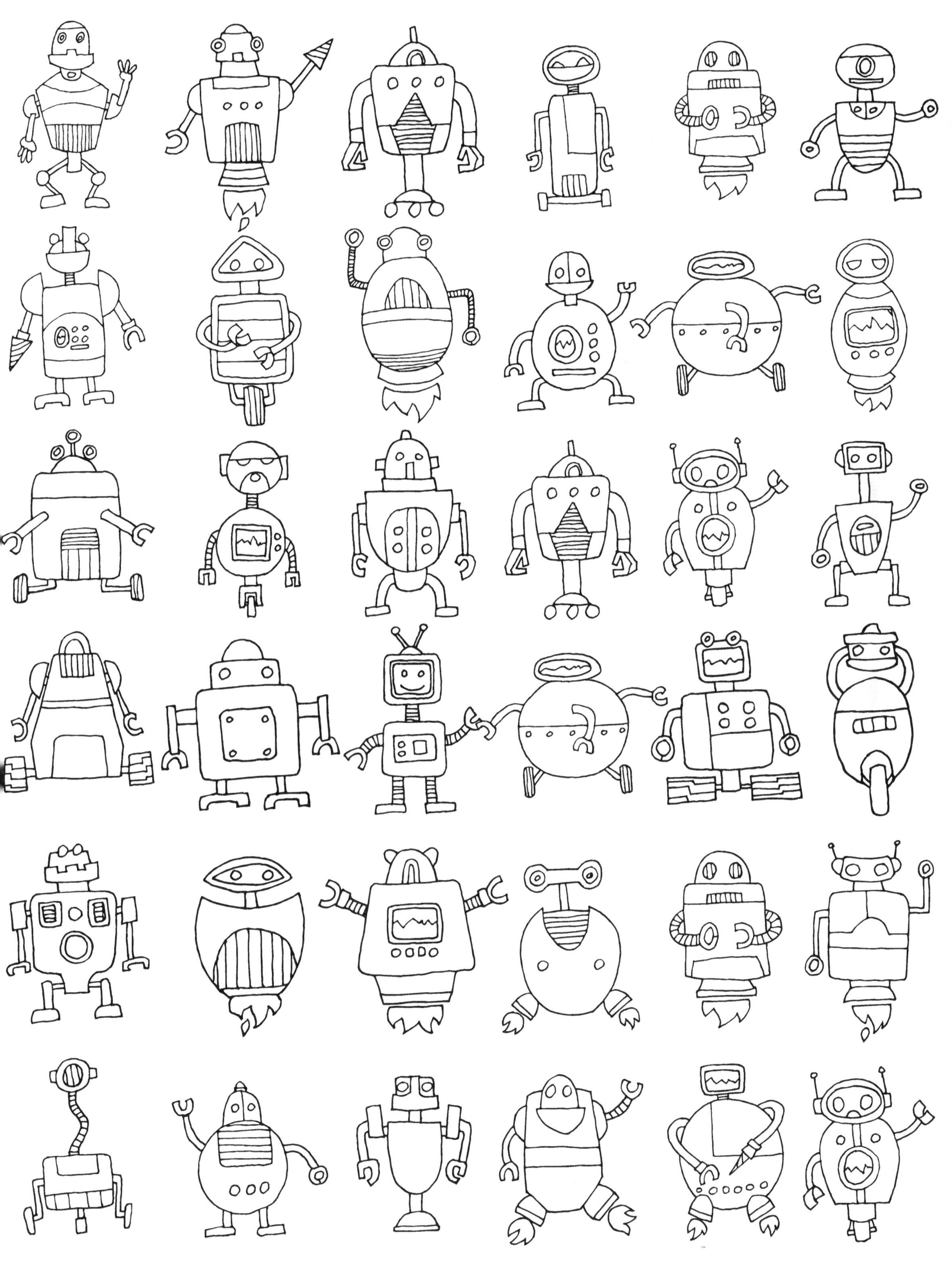

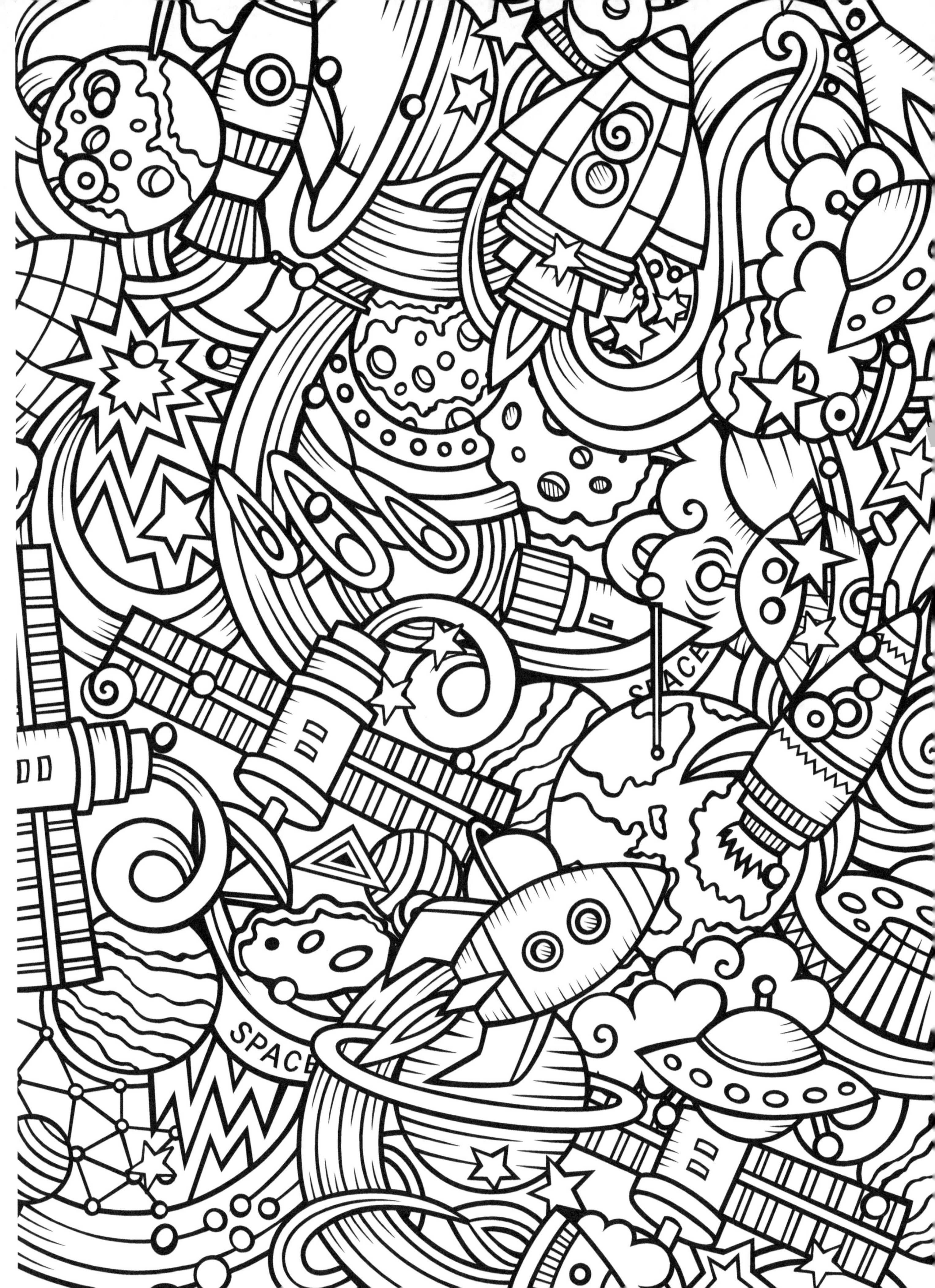
SPACE
SPACE

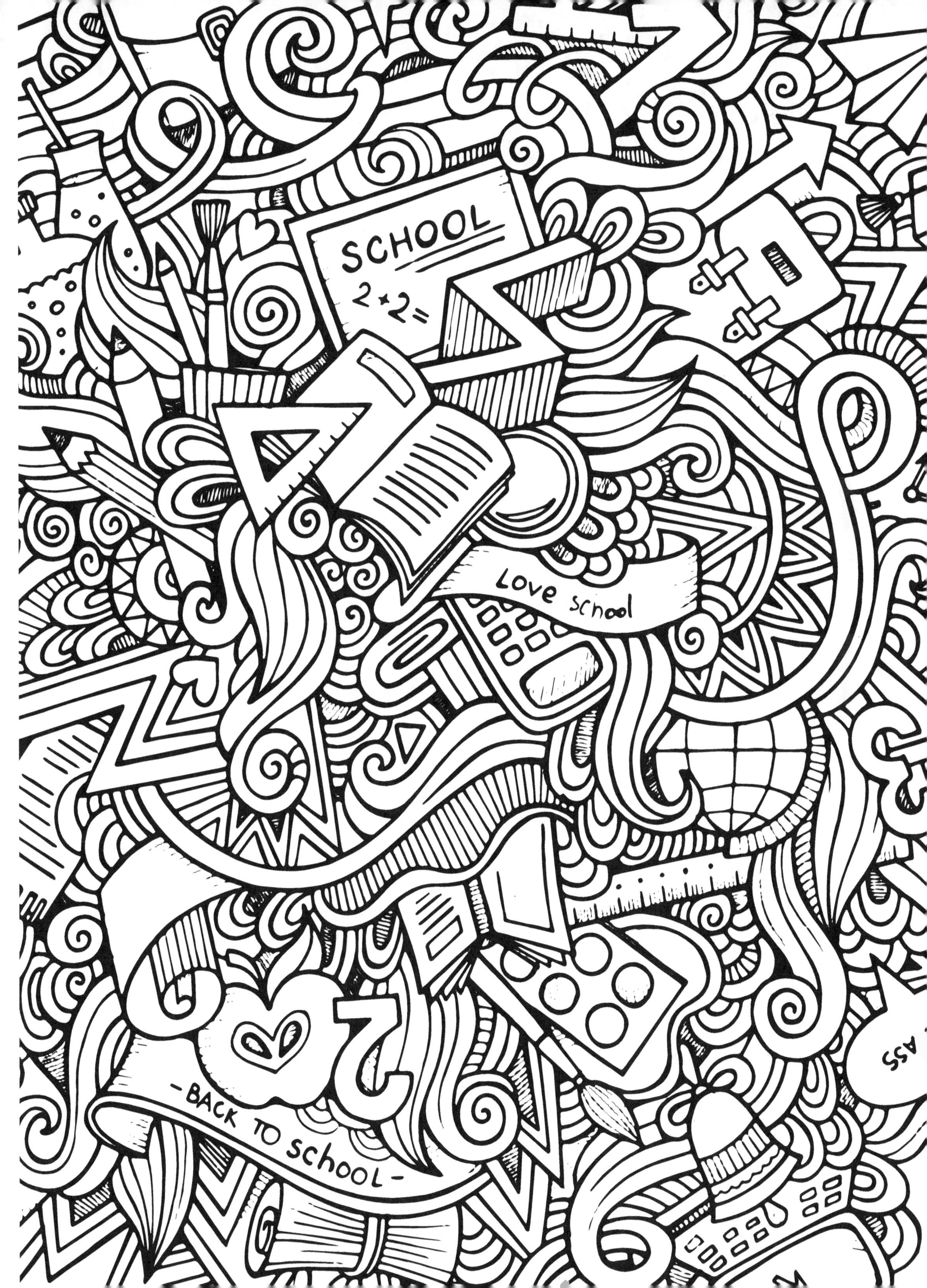
SCHOOL
2+2=
Love School
-BACK TO SCHOOL-

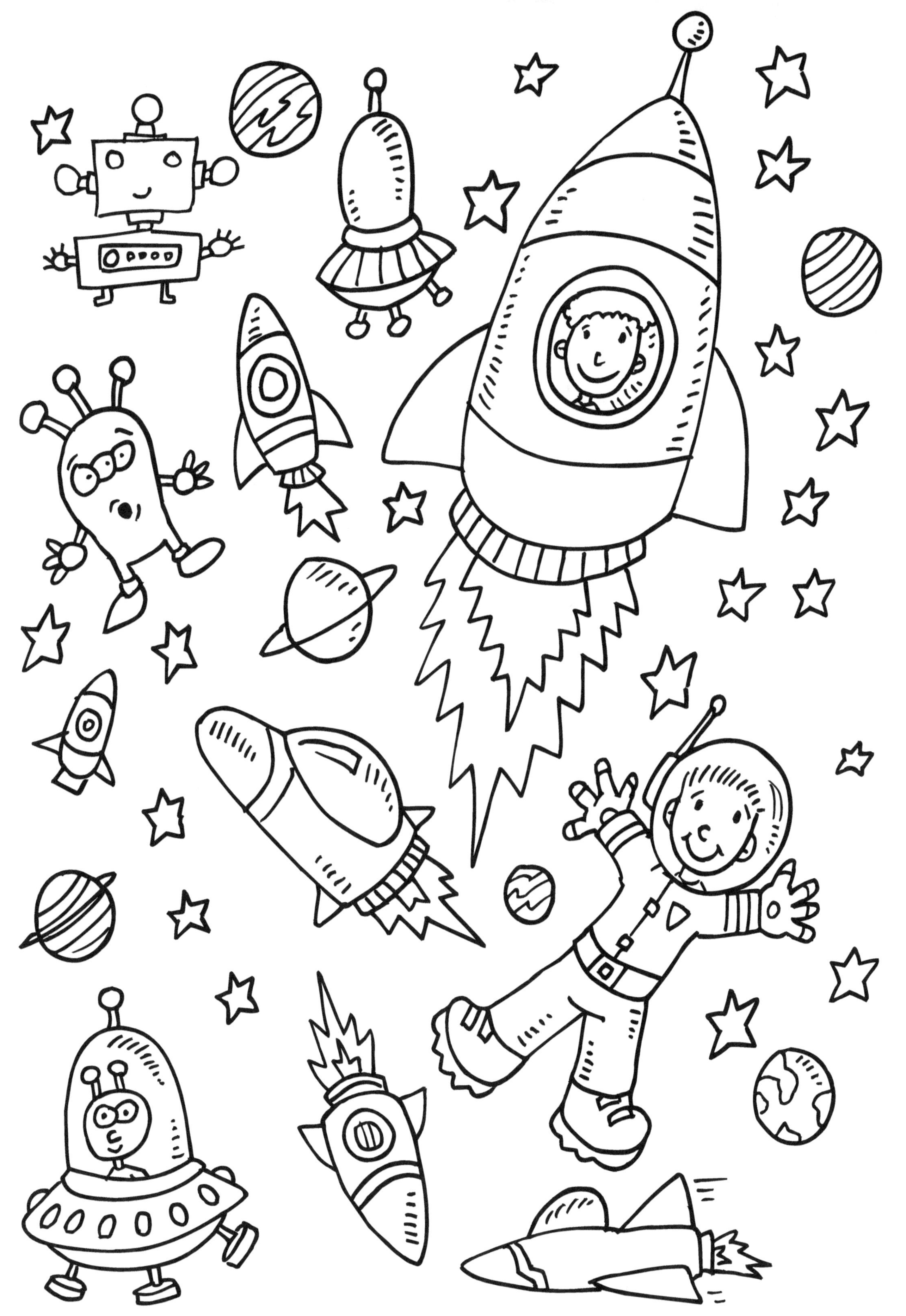

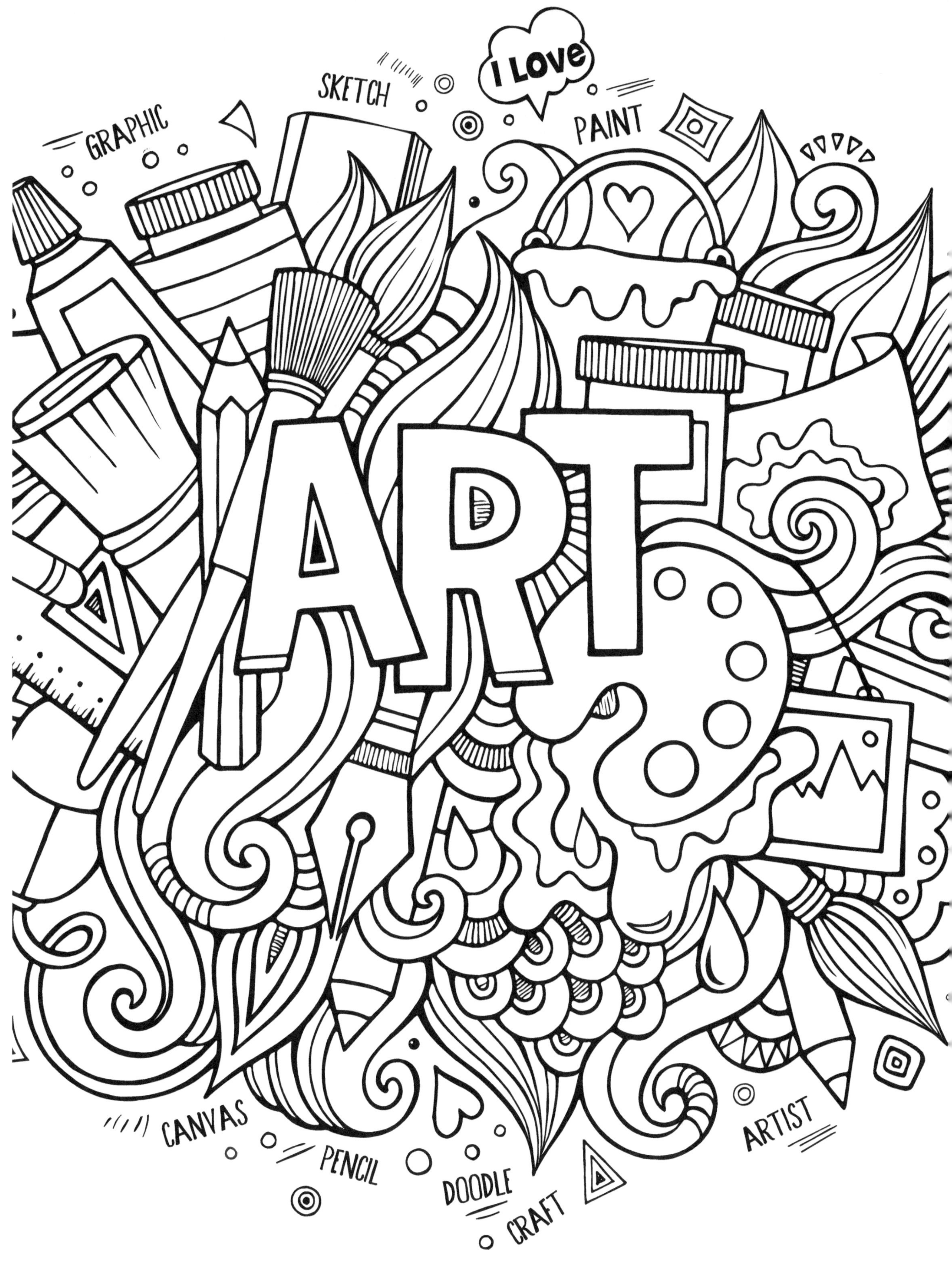
I Love
SKETCH
GRAPHIC
PAINT
ART
CANVAS
PENCIL
DOODLE
CRAFT
ARTIST

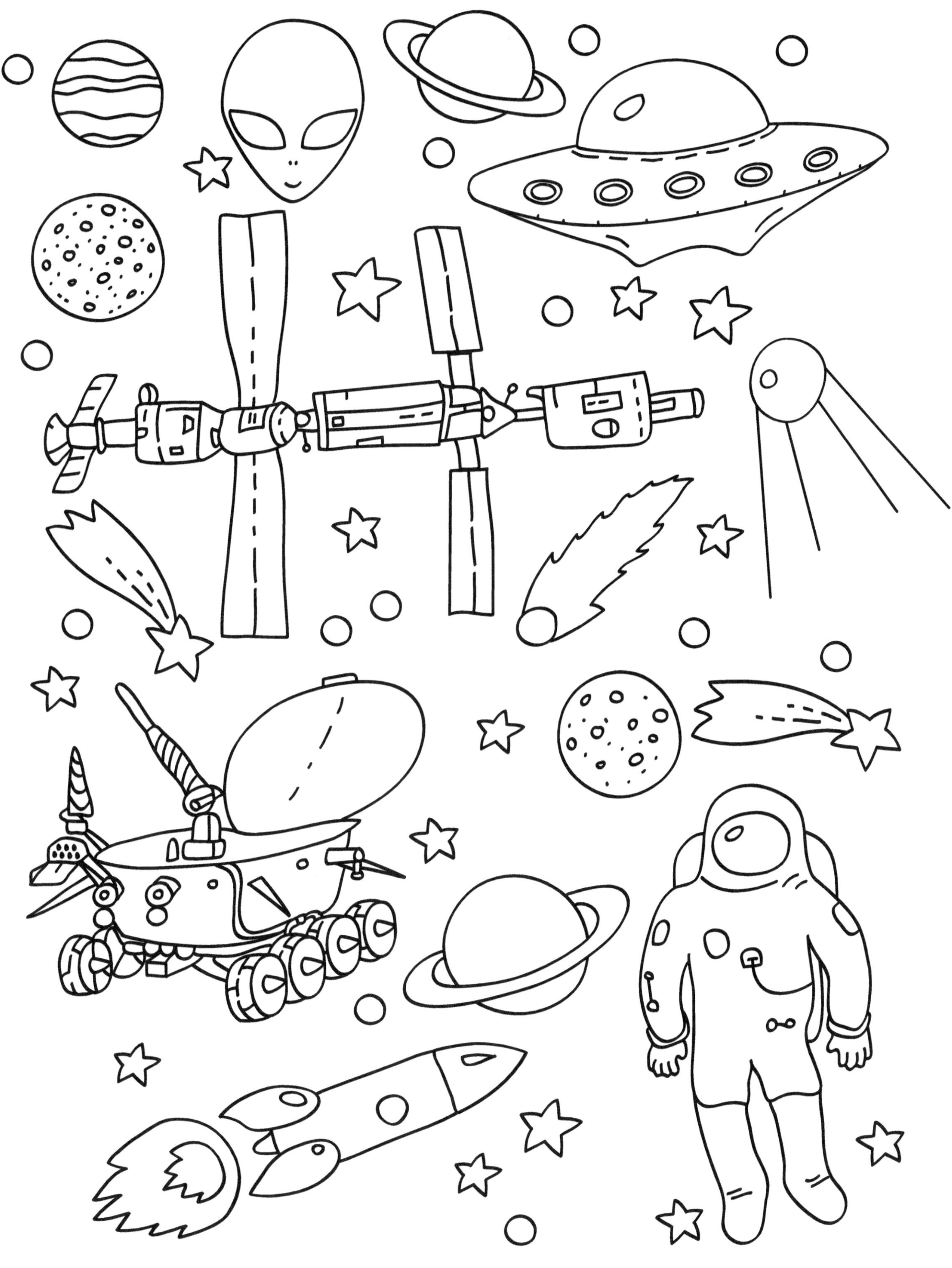

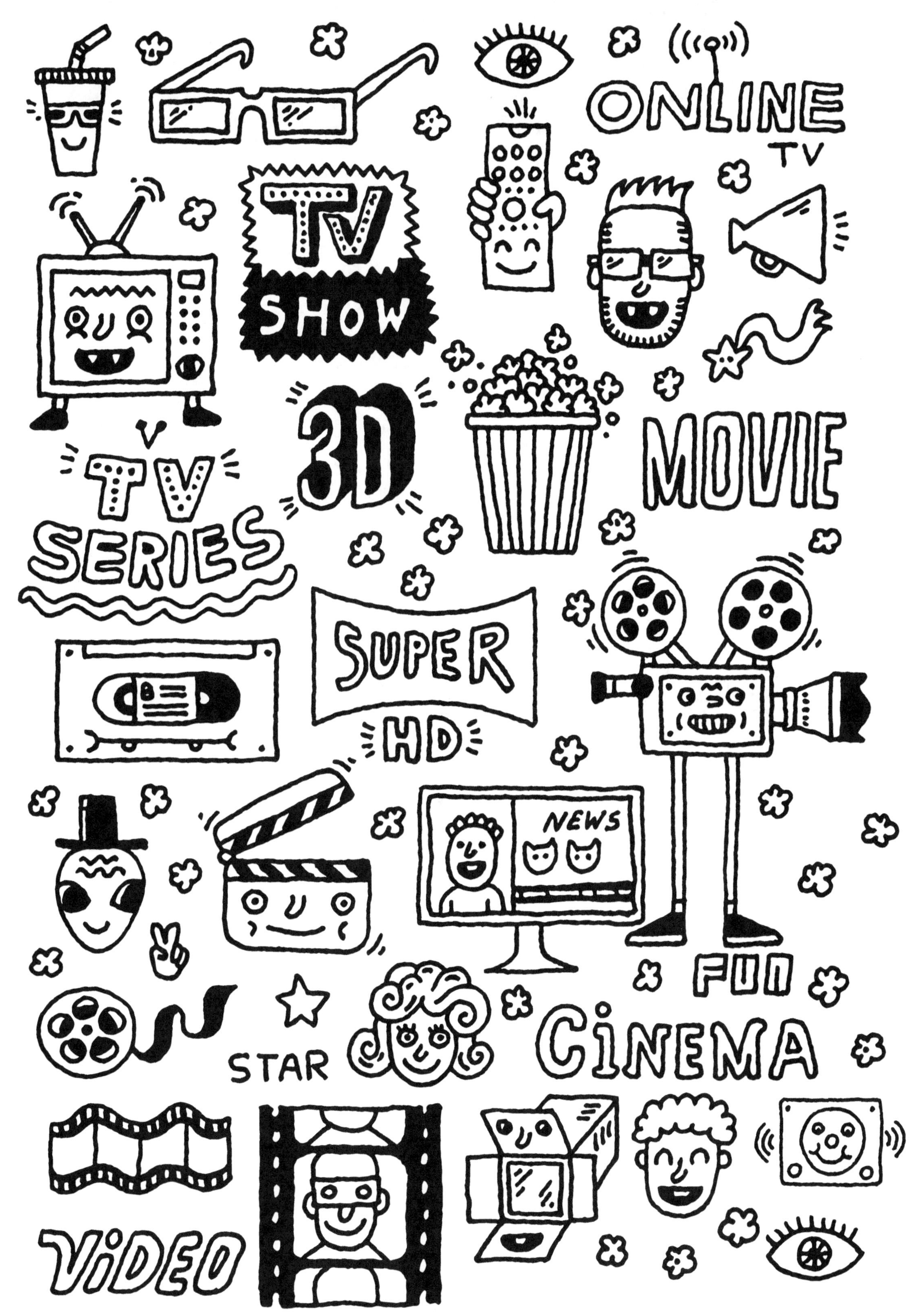

ONLINE
TV
TV
SHOW
3D
MOVIE
TV
SERIES
SUPER
HD
NEWS
FUN
STAR
CiNEMA
ViDEO

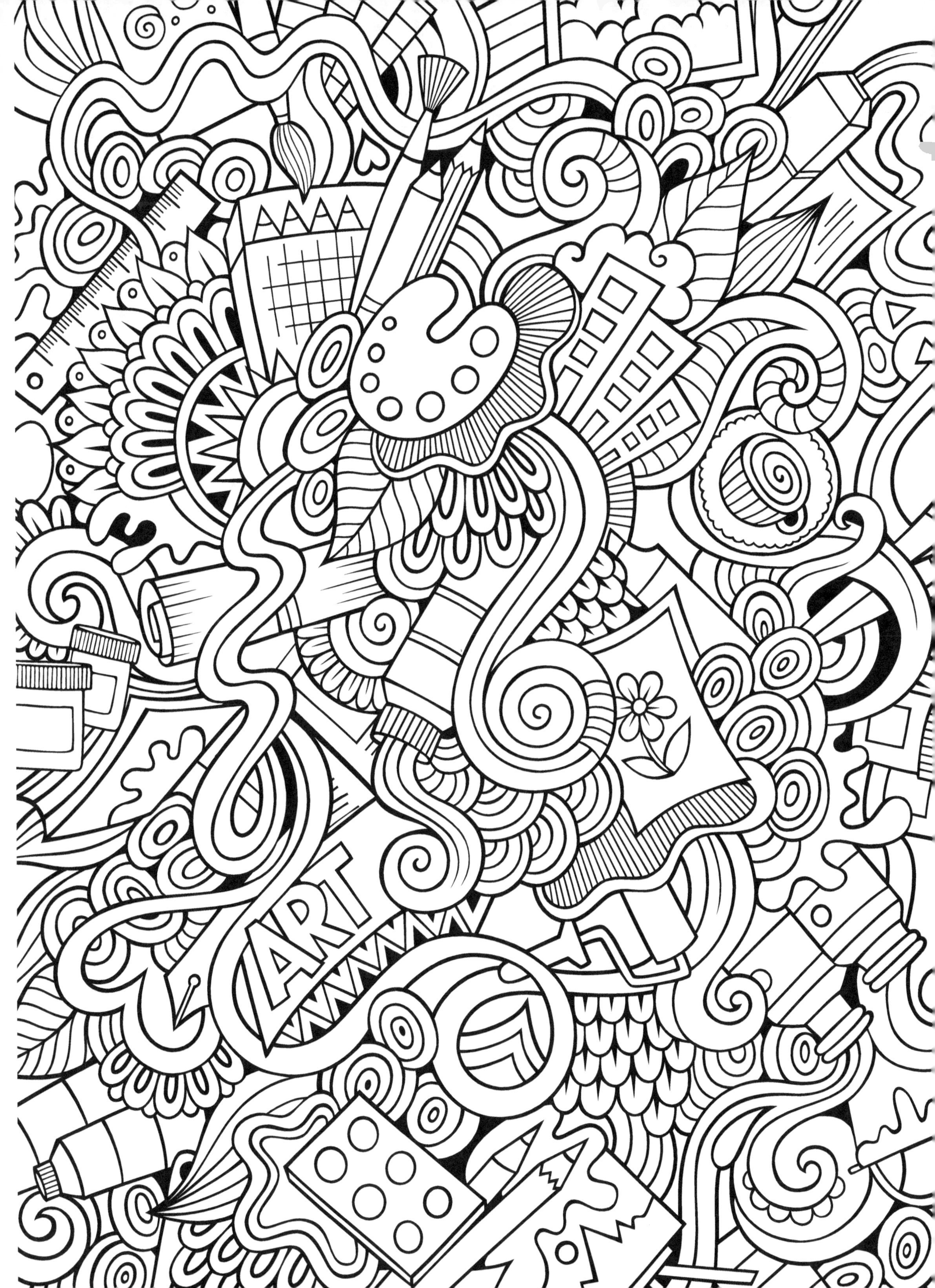
ART

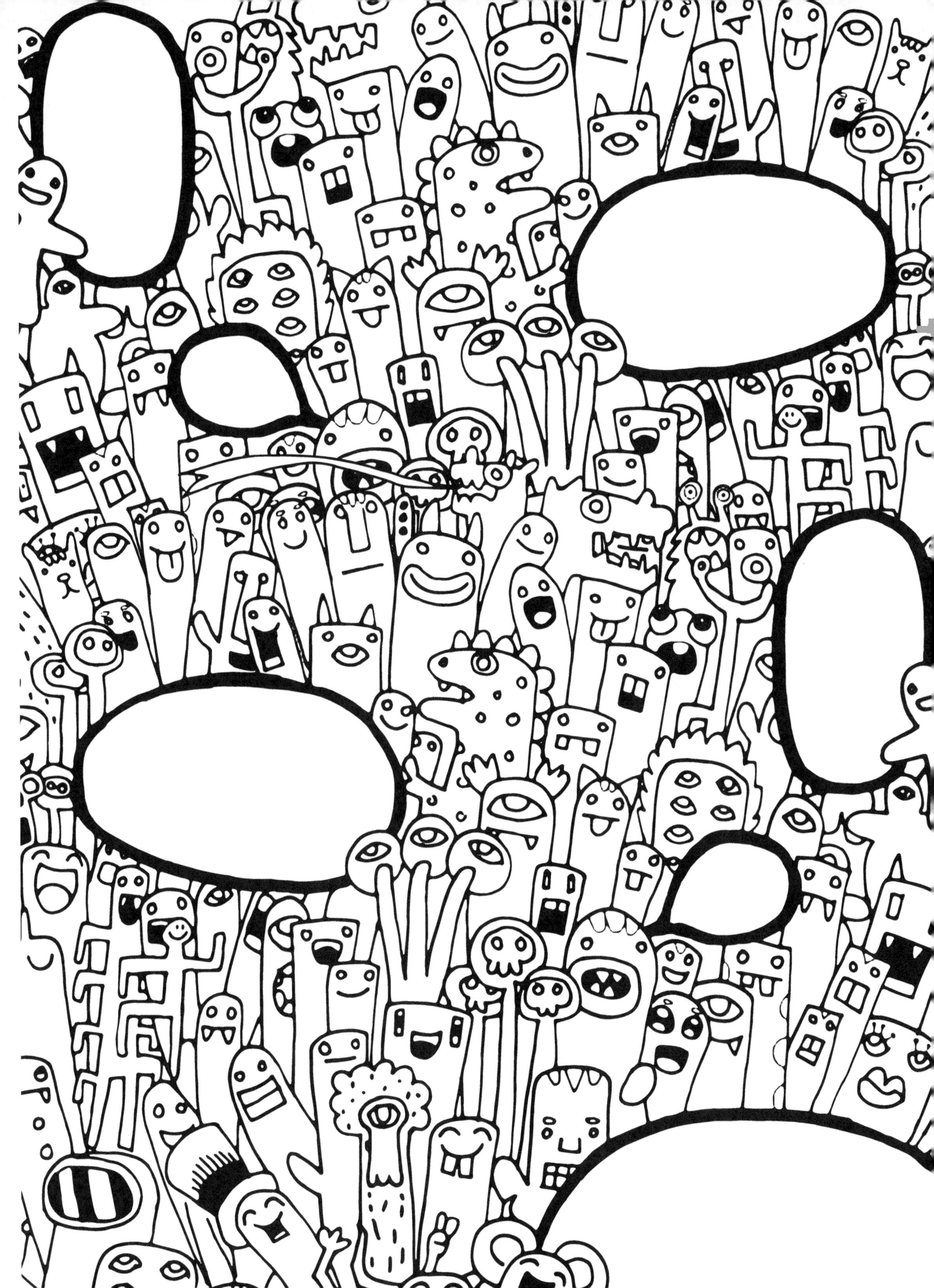

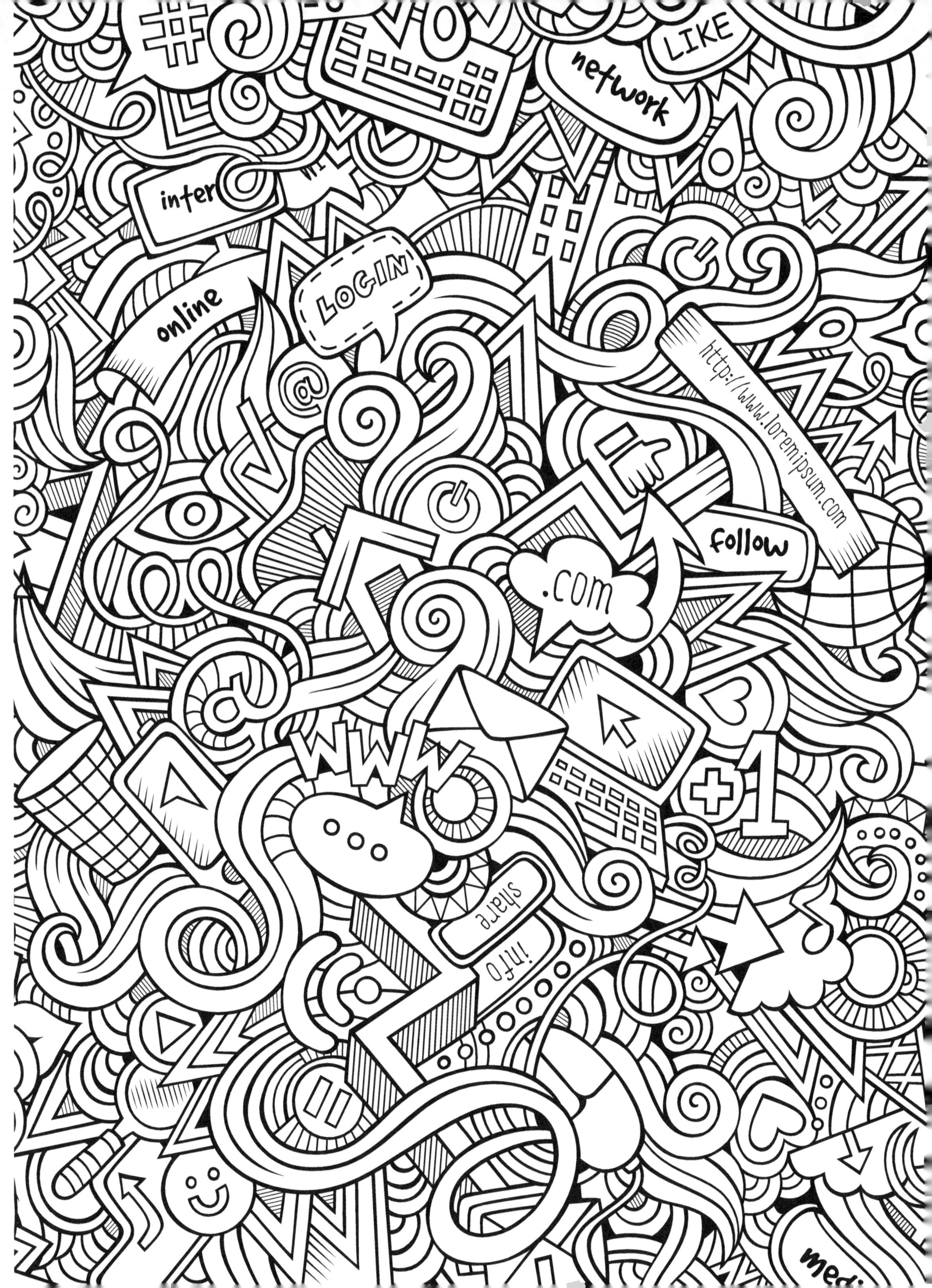
LIKE
network
inter
LOGIN
online
http://www.loremipsum.com
follow
.com
www
+1
share
info

ART
SUPER
ART

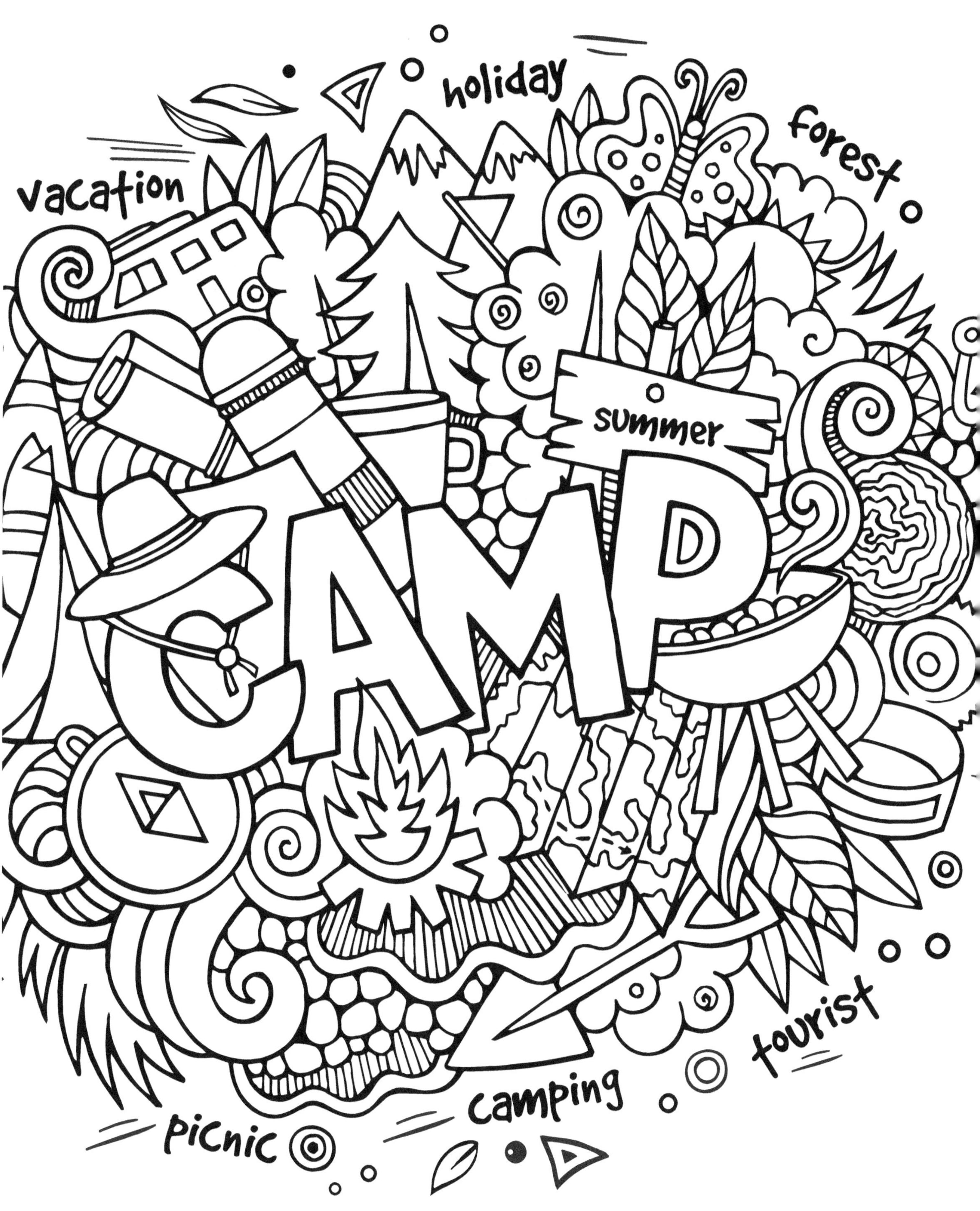
holiday
vacation
forest
summer
CAMP
tourist
camping
picnic

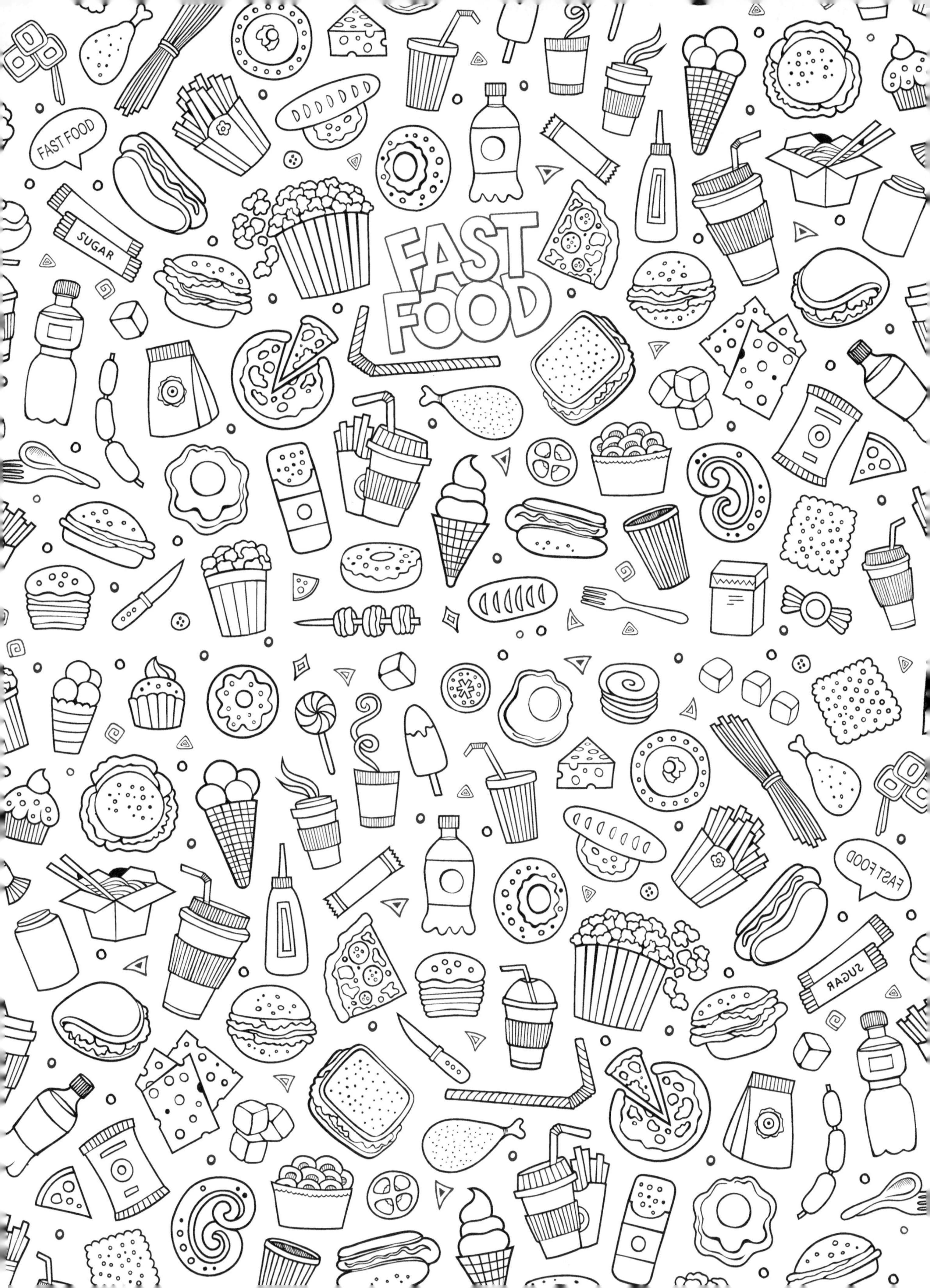
FAST FOOD
FAST FOOD
SUGAR
FAST FOOD
SUGAR

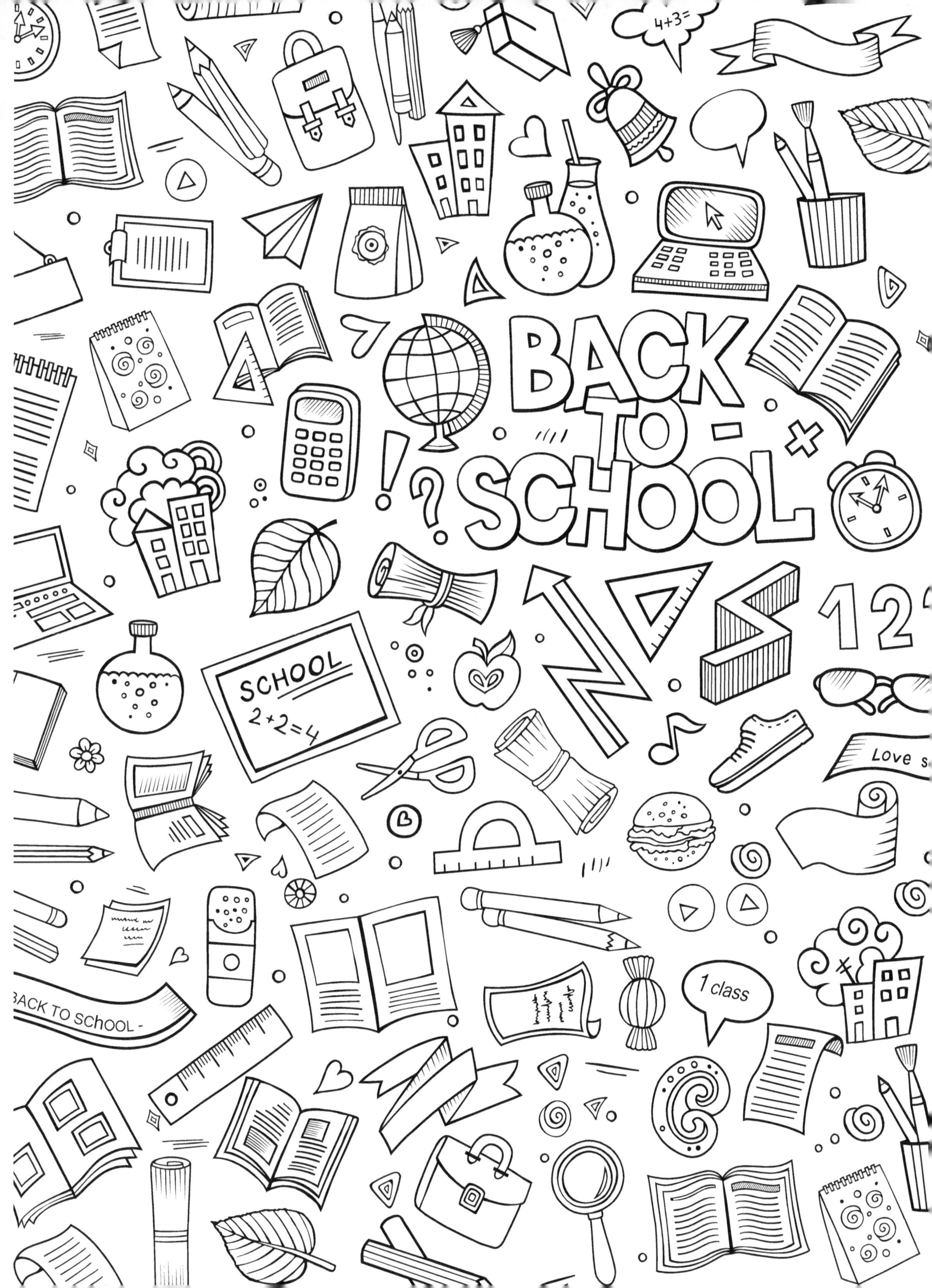
4+3=
BACK TO - SCHOOL
SCHOOL
2+2=4
12
Love s
1 class
BACK TO SCHOOL -

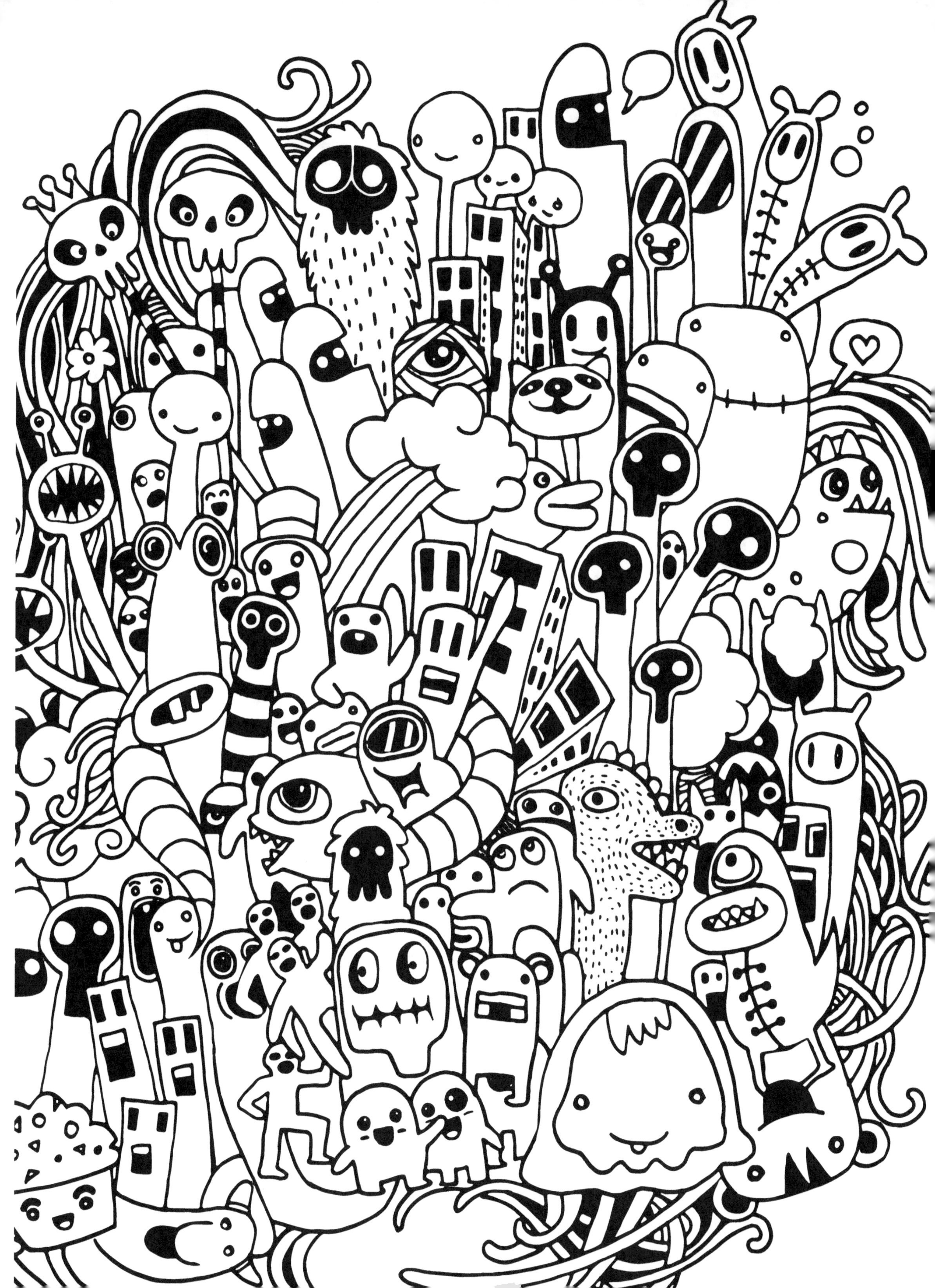

HAPPY
HALLOWEEN
BOO
31
HALLOWEEN
BOO
31

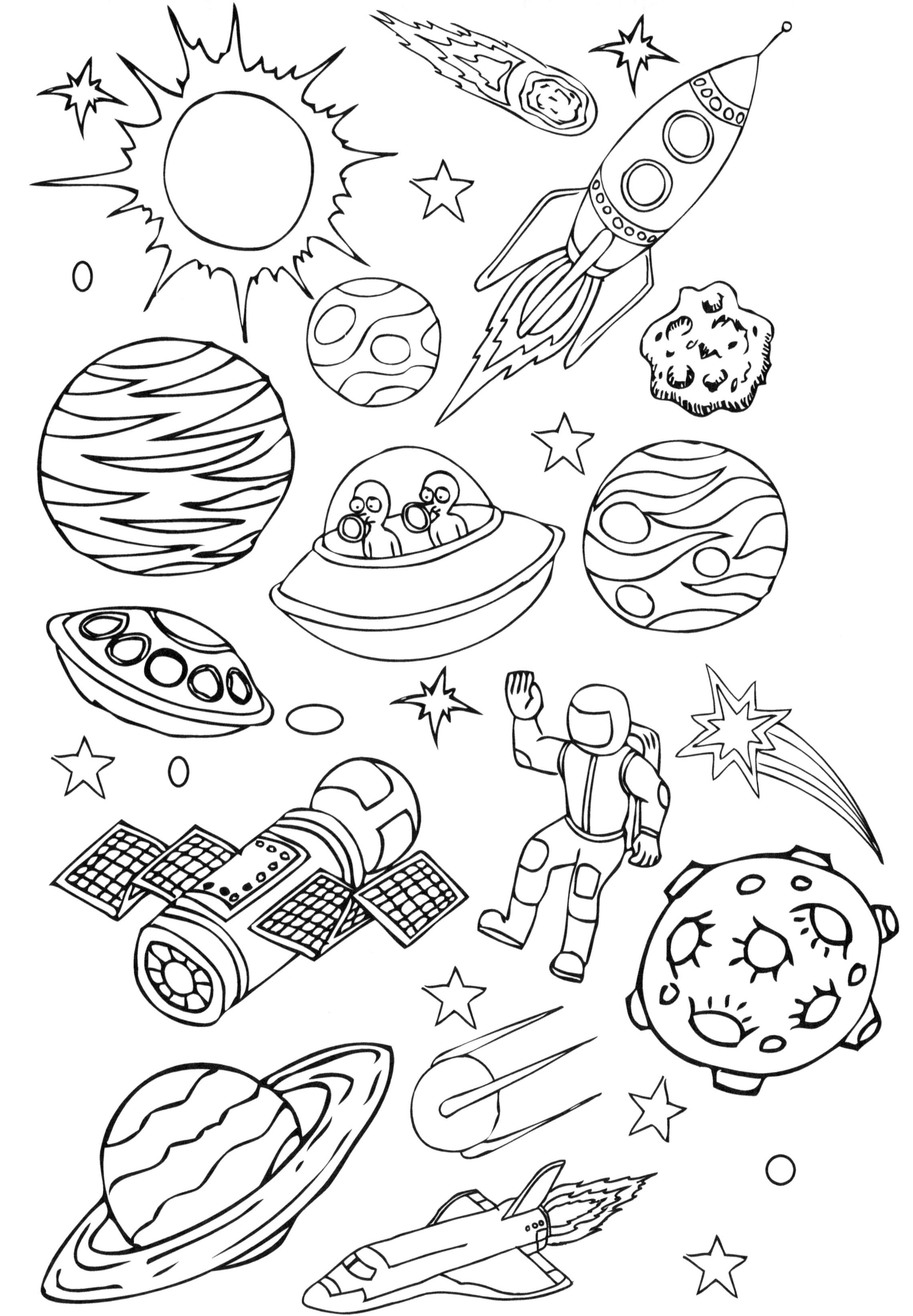

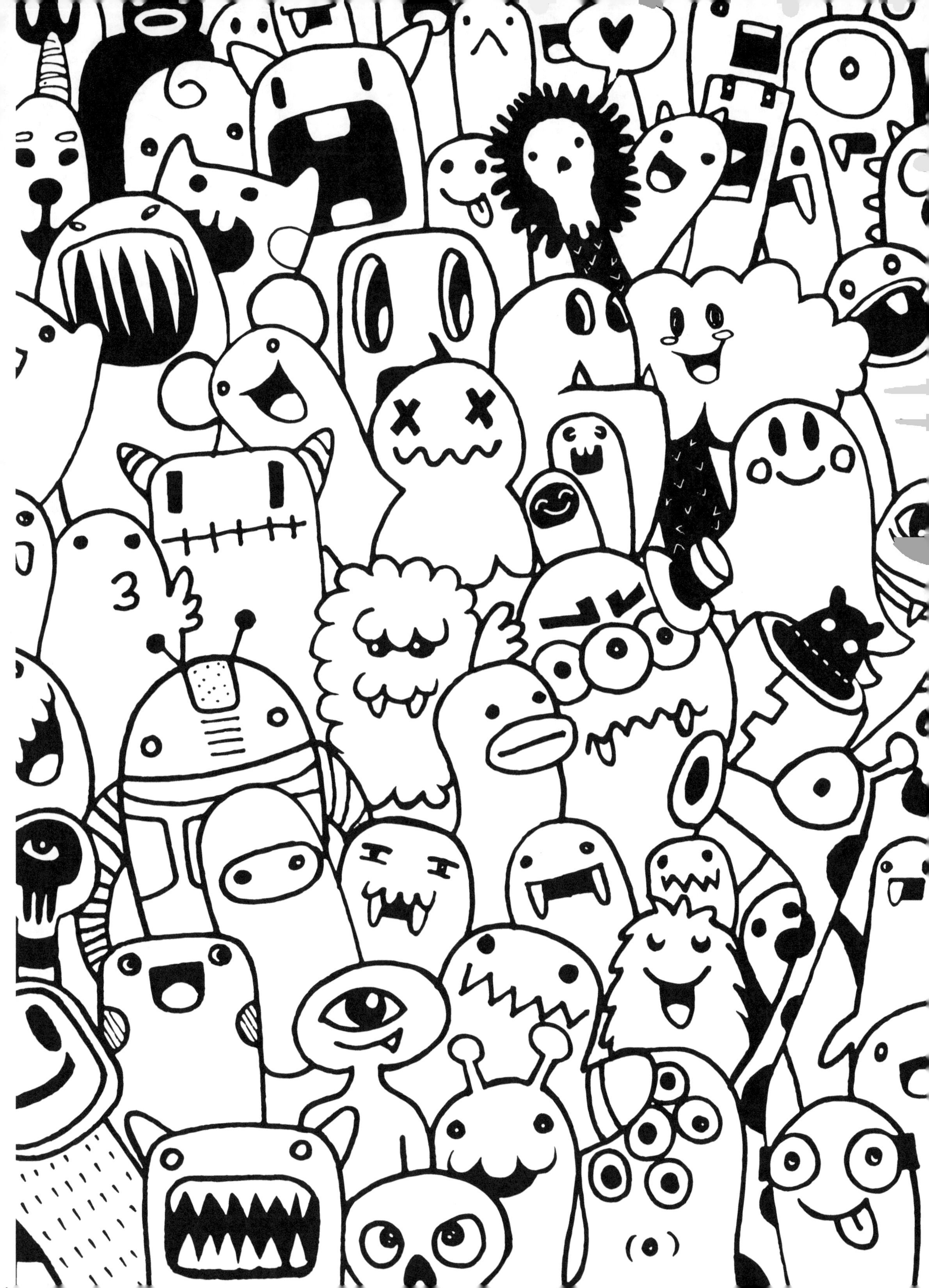

Yo-ho-ho!
ARR
PIRATES!
RUM
Ahoy!

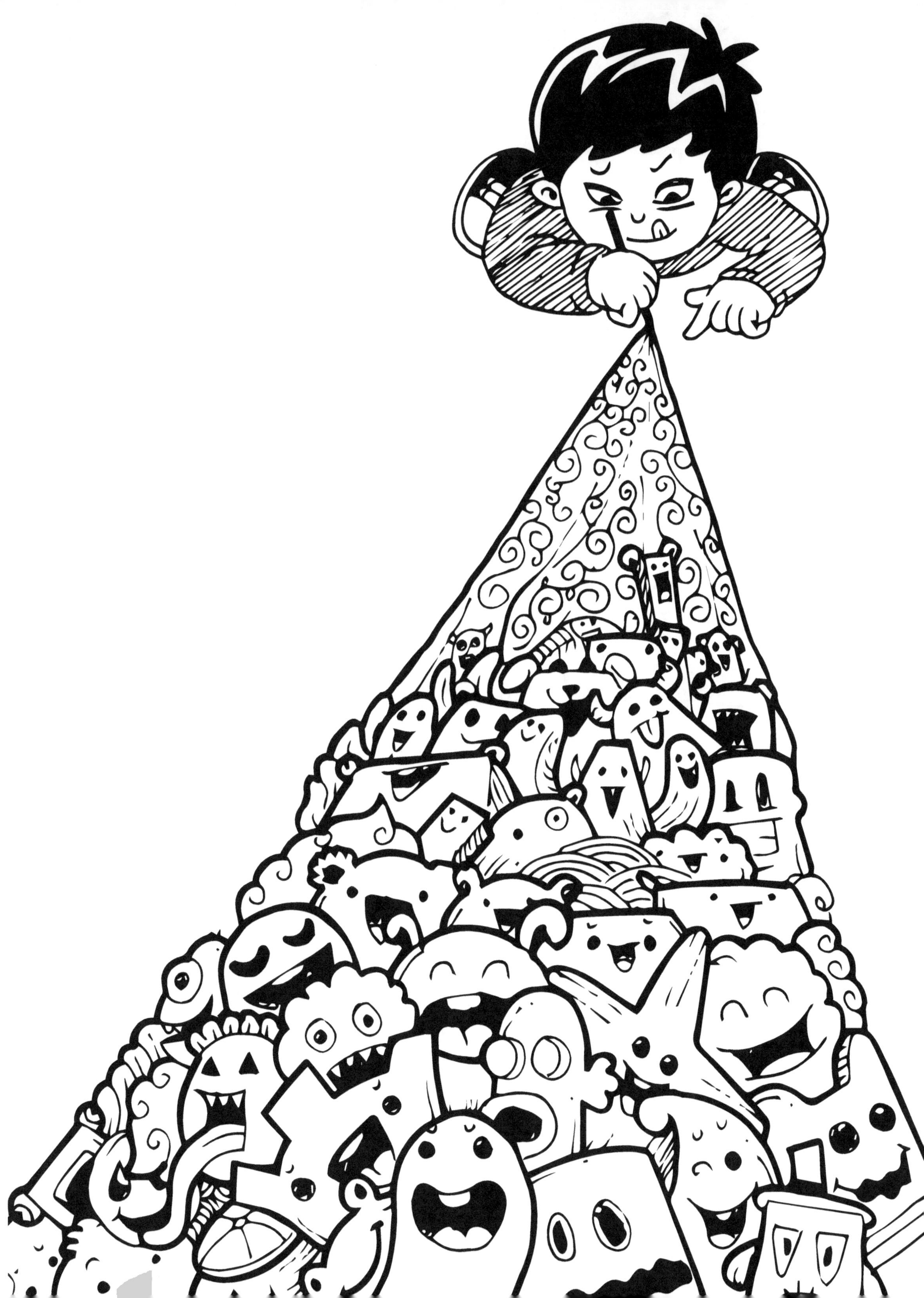

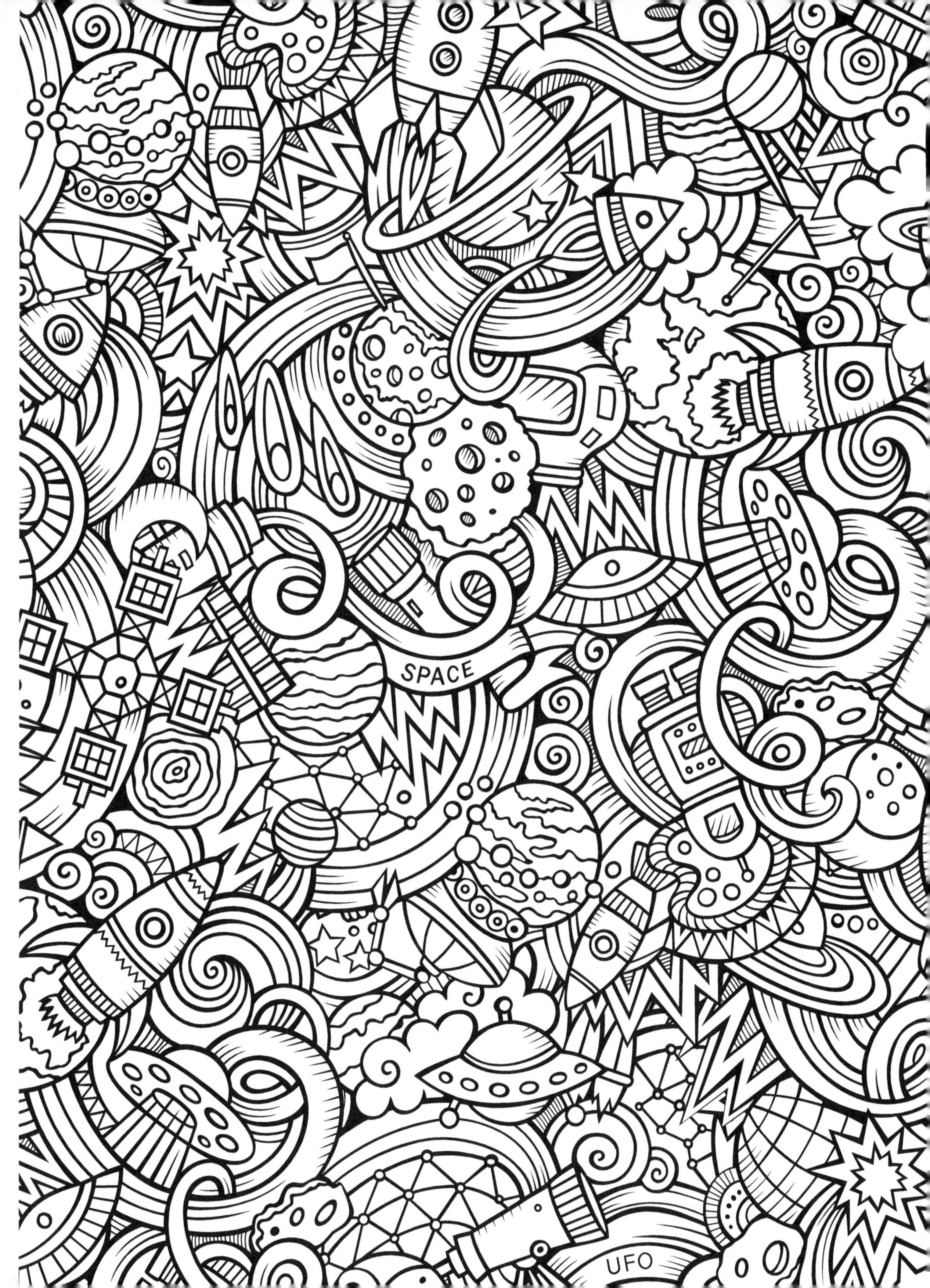
SPACE
UFO

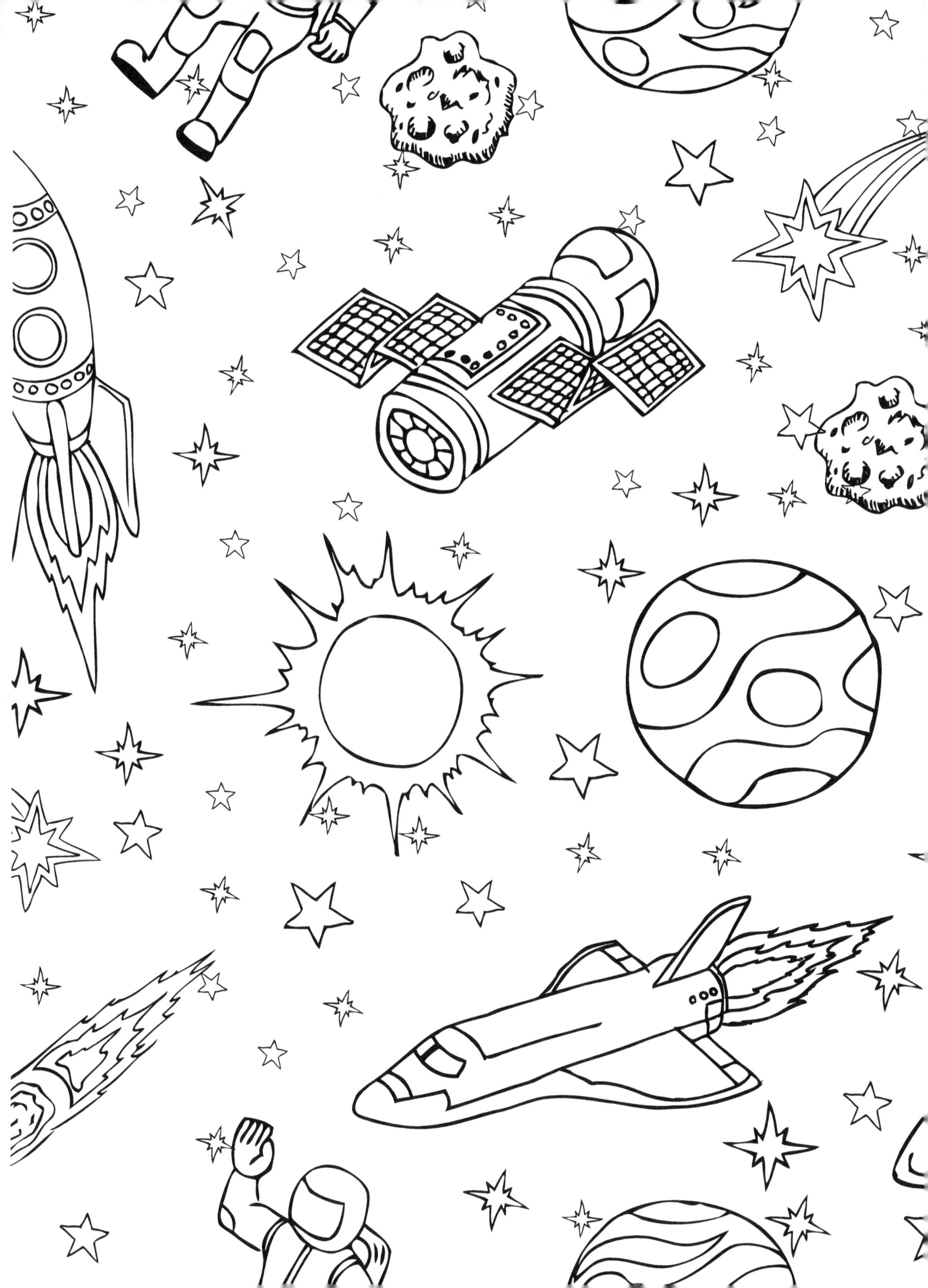

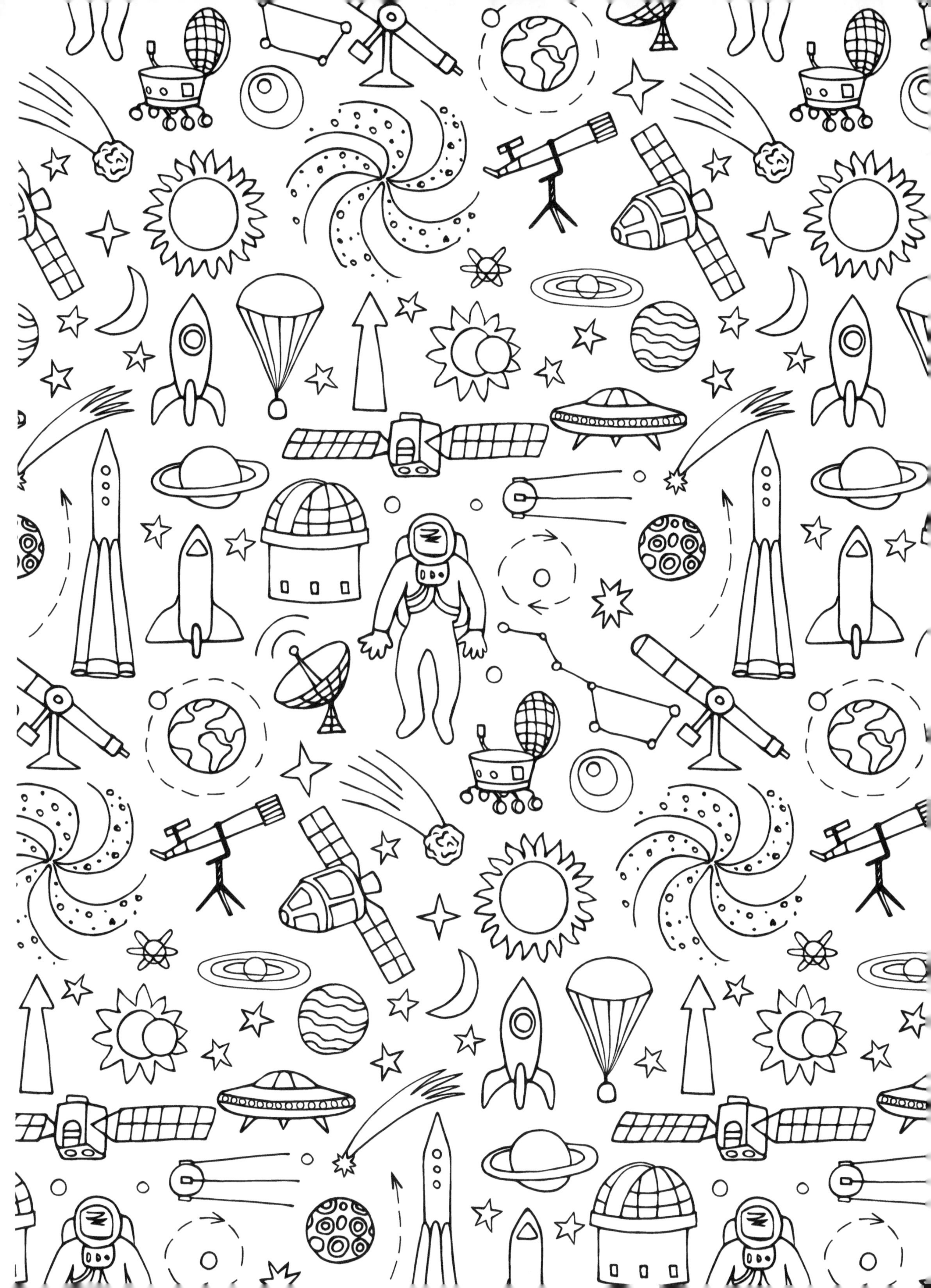

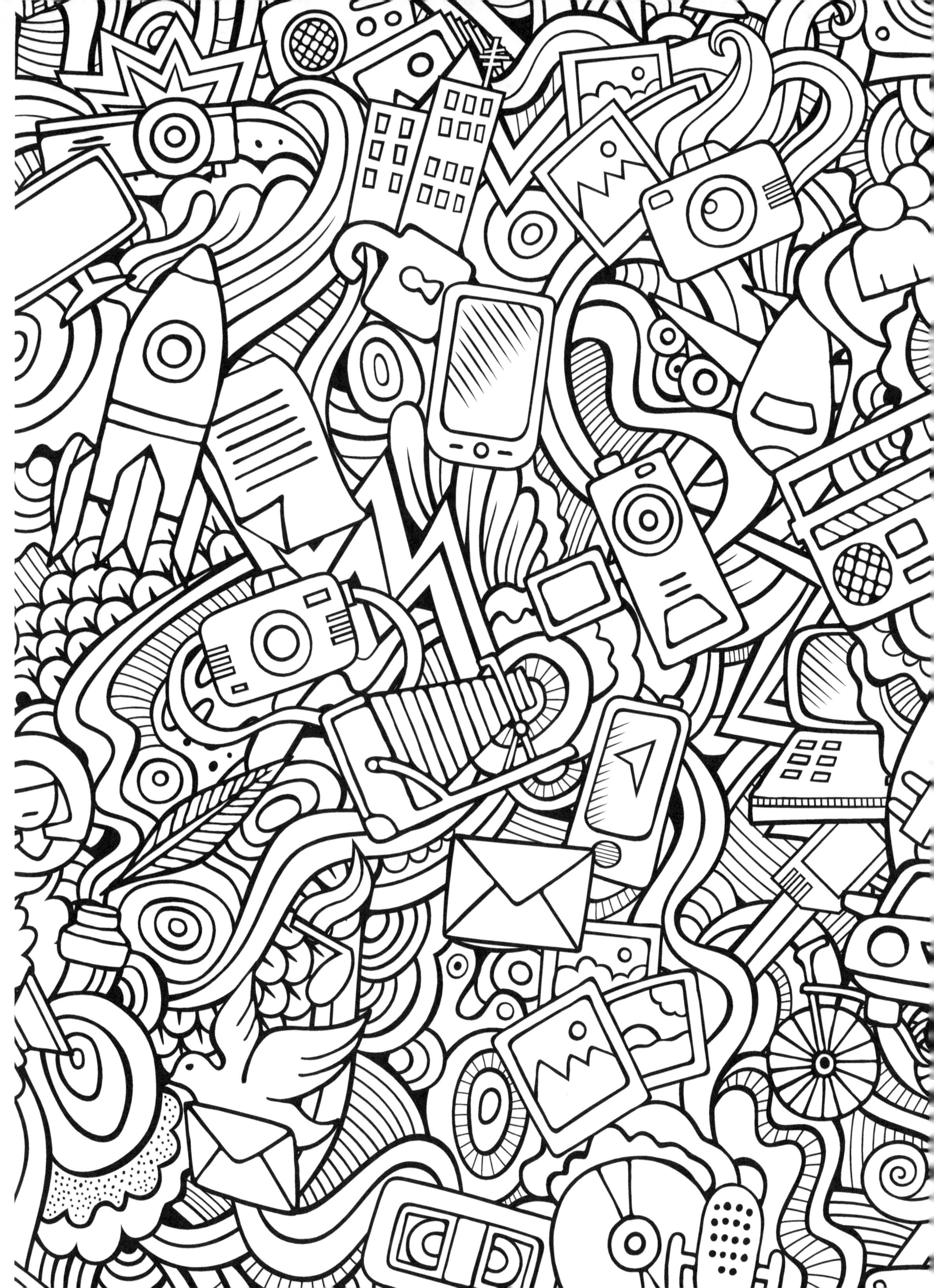

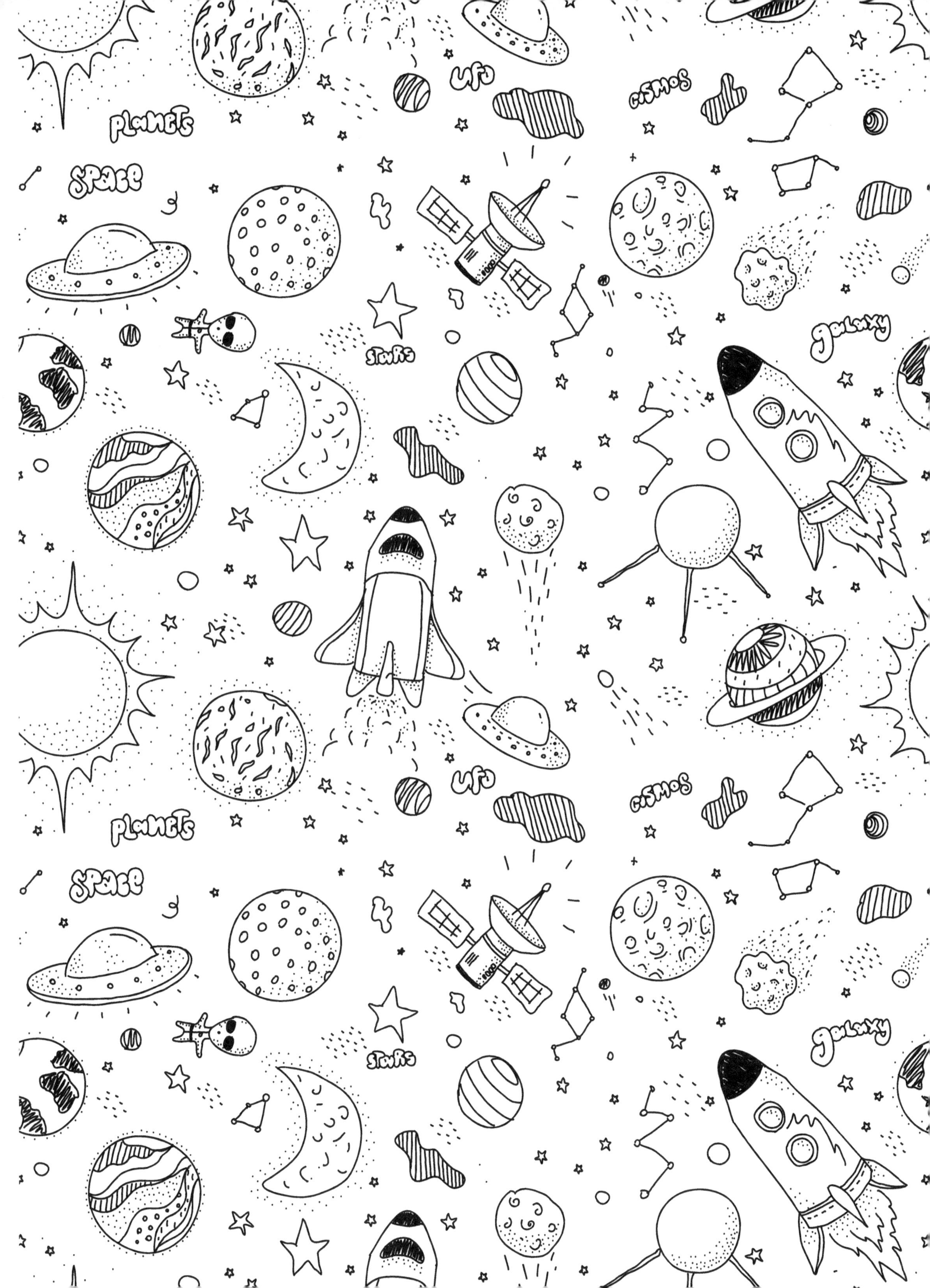

planets
ufo
cosmos
space
stars
galaxy

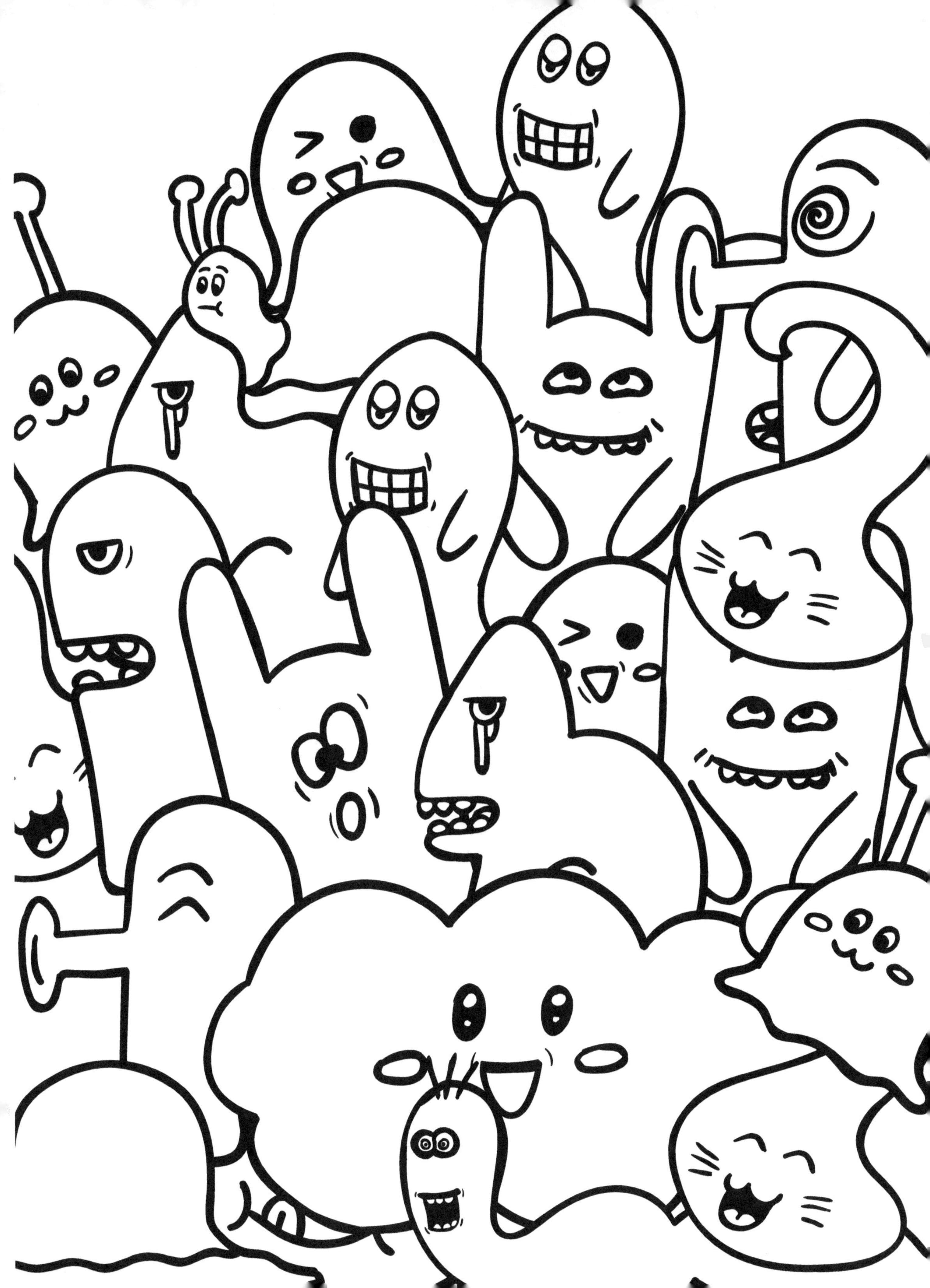

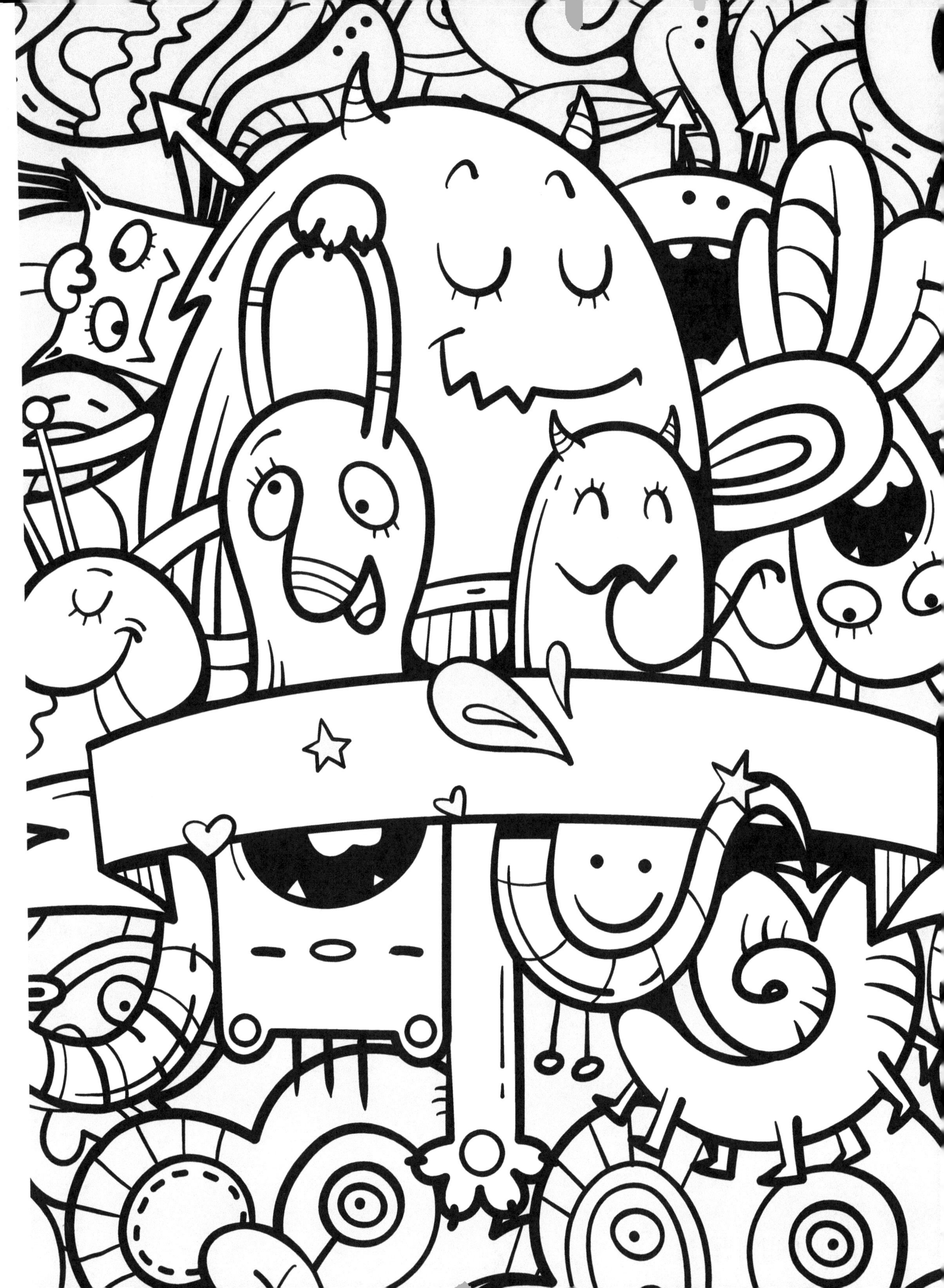

www.ingramcontent.com/pod-product-compliance
Lightning Source LLC
LaVergne TN
LVHW061255100826
845148LV00008B/1133

* 9 7 8 1 7 8 5 9 5 1 2 6 8 *